The Lower Reaches

The
Lower
Reaches

Martin Anderson

Shearsman Books

First published in the United Kingdom in 2013 by
Shearsman Books
50 Westons Hill Drive
Emersons Green
Bristol
BS16 7DF

www.shearsman.com

ISBN 978-1-84861-311-9

Cover drawing: *Fobbing Harbour* by Donald Maxwell,
originally published in his book, *A Detective in Essex* (1933).

"This is England, and I'm in a nice, clean English room with all the dirt swept under the bed".
—Jean Rhys

ONE

I

After the high pitched whine of bellicosity: "We'll bomb you back to the stone age" the remote is pressed. Crackle of distressed air. Warm, incendiary smell. All colour implodes to a white mote. Silence. The crevasse opens.

II

Boiling white spume. Caught on steps of the public baths before noon, the shadow of a vapour. Ash, in the dissolved hand. Shard, or ember. All melted into air. In the stone, heart's cold memento.

III

What keel breaks this ice? What *dignitas* is affirmed in these particulars of a profound winter? Our Lady of the Salterns bless this rotting wharf, this ramshackle back-end deserted by the tides. It is snowing over all the reed clogged wet-lands of the earth.

IV

Scent of sea asters edging the creek. "Die Tankanlagen" under the aimer's sight. "Marschland." Identified/located from a great height. Locked in a grid: "Zu den Sachen Selbst!" Held for a moment in his gaze, they bleed. Blackened viscera. The air receives them.

V

"Perched on the rotten shell of a crumbling empire." He writhed. Listening to its long, inhaled sighs. A continent in trouble, economies adrift. Bemused at its beleaguered identity. Its 'cradle' mocked by its own hand. Not a 'Hellenic Occident' (extending east of the Dardanelles) no. No, surely. But an acropolis purged of the stain of all jewelled, scented potentates. Austere. White: its *demokratia*, its *logos*. Derided now and held up as dishonest, its people indolent. And, held up instead as its antithesis, those hardworking lands which provided souls for the Middle Passage and whose people previously they'd characterised as "lazy beasts [who] must be compelled to work—with a stick" … and "whether they should be reckoned as beings of the same species." Perched on that rotten shell he "received such a salutation in [his] nostrils as [he] had never experienced in [his] life."

VI

Outside the window purple reeded hollows of the former fleet. Sea lavender, grey with river light. At the inlet's mouth, where a "leakinge, unwholesome ship" once harvested wind, tide lapped silt bars catching the sun's last rays ignite. As, too, the scarp's high ledge of flowering thorn—a "Sea-mark", Hawksbury-bush > Hamechesburga > burh: *hill*. The Hill of the Hawks. To navigate a way back, from the farthest corners of the earth.

VII

Togodumnus. Dead or lost amidst the reed beds. Harried from fen to fen. His horses slain. Pursued into the claggy wastes east of the Island of Thorns. Aiming beyond the sand capped wooded heights for Camulodunum, he disappeared. Sound of the bittern booming amid bull rushes. Slither of sword hilt and shield, as each man sought to hold his footing through the miry labyrinth. Water welded to sky. On the salt driven wind the sound of men closing. Panick, then stumbling. A foreign tongue. There is gold in Dalcouthi. There is silver.

VIII

Die Tankanlagen. Over the mudflats the smell of oil. Dream of an ideal order. Beyond any particular geography, any particular time or place at all. Driving men mad. Blacking the shore. Leveraging the sea-lanes open. "A perpetuall warre without peace or truce." Crude. Pungent in summer, over the fields and hedgerows. And in the houses of the villages. Ancient distillate. Of a mind which "(save upward to the heavens) could have little solace or content in respecte of any outward objects." Or any inward excursus at all.

TWO

I

Out of the forlorn city at last, its fogs and its counting houses. The white noise in the rigging after dark. Droning. Insincere. Incessant. Past Thorn Island where one summer the effluvium became too much even for those inside debating. Each voice overlapping and merging with the other. And with those outside, reporting. Downstream. Past Hole Haven. Scent of sea lavender on the breeze. White noise in the rigging. Smell of the open sea roads. Stars look down on another journey about to be undertaken.

II

Struggling through deep drifts with a copy of *Der Angriff* under his arm, a latter day Robert Conway. Ice fragments from the Pontic steppes lodged deep in the tread of his boots, his shadow survives in abattoirs and in the stockyards of railway terminuses. In the frozen breath of *die Kristallnacht*. But who has not followed and extolled, through a bloodied swathe of foreign villages and towns, that small red rowan on his cheek, "that nobly arched head, containing such a quantity of brain… those coral lips?"

III

Driftway, sluice. Beyond, breakwater, river scour, margin. Where foreland of saltern is over-lapped. "All overflowen." And eyot, and terp: "quite drowned." No tithe map of any use. No tiltboat to stairs or wharf. Undrained. Unforded. What soggy track, inter-coursed with copse/willow, to follow? All wetland words, and ways, converge; seem foreign. To find a way, amid shifting brine sump, piling, hollow.

IV

Togodumnus. Feet in mud. Following the channel's curve.
Seeking the higher ground. Above the sedge lapped verge his
shadow flits. Gulls cry out over the sunken tideway. Revenge.
But there are no tracks to guide him back. Each imprint erased
in the flood's quiet launder.

V

For "a pug nosed rodent with lustrous fur", for a pile of moth eaten pelts, the "beaver fields exhausted", the great Eastern deciduous forest depleted, a civilisation, with no concept of wealth accumulation, "debauched"; bodies "washed up on the lawns of the [ ] consulate in Surabaya ... rivers jammed with [them] like logs": for a "cheap little creed".

VI

Shiver and sweat of tidewrack. Limbs blue. Cold flicker on silt
bank. Slippage of foot, glissando. Through Flat and Ooze where
the river "enters the Ocean"—"carelessly camped upon its
bank". *In avia secutus*. Head spun. Heart colder. To bend, finally,
at Claudius' foot. Not dead. A survivor. REG MAG IN BRIT.
An instrument, *reges et amici*, of the imperium. Benefactor, and
supporter, of an ideal order.

VII

Sun dappled worm-eaten wharf in a wilderness of water and sky. Where the "aguish miasma" rose after sun dip. Where the starch collared pilot set out under the sand capped scarp. Light on hedge bank, on fill dyke. To guide far off destinies afloat through treacherous shoals, sands. For a country intent, at any cost, on extending its reach. *Oppidum.* Power point. Wooden pile driven into the mud. The lap of distant climes against it.

VIII

'Big swinging dicks' amid the rigging. All hands below aloft chipping ice off a top heavy vessel. The ice-master frantic. All Libor rates 'fixed'. "A… culture rotten with cynicism and greed." "A cesspit." Scent of sea lavender on the breeze. From the Hill of the Hawks what eye looks down?

IX

A journey endlessly postponed. In the leather lined clubs of its capital. At regattas, tattoos and royal enclosure. In "cultivate[d] nostalgia". In the Honours list nailed to the door. In expurgated diaries of heros who "swear all day at [their] companions" and are transformed into "splendid failure[s]". In 'lost' government archives. In the inherited and laundered loot of families and State. In a mythos of fairness assiduously cultivated and disposed. By an emasculated corps of vendors of 'news'. By a plethora of anointed insouciants … Fractured identity. Full of unopened doors. "Profound hypocrisy". Of lives too comfortable and safe to force the locks, and look. At that feted image. At that camera obscura of themselves.

X

From le Hole havene, "in very deep and current free water at maximum practicable distance from the coast … the files … in weighted crates", *And specially from every shires ende / Of Engelond … they wende* past gut and hedgebank, creekside and shore, on "perambulation", prayers offered en route, pollard "bounds trees" freshly scored or mutilated, on occasion youths ceremoniously scourged so they would remember a significant location, "by the time I cut his balls off … he had no ears and his eyeball, the right one, I think, was hanging out of its socket", mapping the "Bounds of the parish". Three and a half tons of what "might embarrass" the government, and "whose existence … should never be revealed." Scent of sea lavender over the mud. "…he died before we got much out of him". Smell of the open sea roads.

XI

Our Lady of the Salterns bless this rotting wharf, this ramshackle
back-end deserted by the tides.

NOTES

ONE

I: "We'll bomb...", Pakistan's President Musharraf, BBC television interview, 2006. Threat made to him by US official. [First used by American General Curtis LeMay in 1968, in relation to N. Vietnam.]

IV: "Die...", from target photographs of Thameshaven oil refineries issued to Luftwaffe aircrews during WWII.
"Zu den...", Edmund Husserl, *Logische Untersuchungen*, 1900/01. [We must turn to the things themselves!—Rather than, as in Kant, the mystical thing-in-itself.]

V: "Perched...", Ezra Pound, *The New Age*, 1913.
"Dishonest ..", Christine Lagarde, Head of the IMF, *The Guardian* 25th May 2012: paraphrase of.
"lazy beasts ..", Sir Rudolph Slatin of the Soudan, quoted by F. W. Hurst in *Liberalism and the Empire*, 1900.
"whether they...", *Memoirs*, Catherine Cappe, 1823.
"received such...", Olaudah Equiano, a black slave quoted by John M. Hobson in *The Eastern Origins of Western Civilisation*: "I was soon put down under the decks...". Dysentery and dehydration meant the deck, according to a contemporary ship's surgeon, "was so covered in blood and mucus ... it resembled a slaughterhouse".

VI: "leakinge, unwholesome ..", John Smith, *The Generall History of Virginia, New England, and the Summer Isles*, 1624: Smith's description is of the *Mayflower*.
"Sea-mark", Randal Bingley, *Fobbing: Essays on an Essex Parish*.

VII: Togodumnus: a king of the Catuvellauni in southern England who, in a battle described as one of the most important in English history and which took place between present day East Tilbury and Stanford-le-Hope, resisted the Roman invasion/occupation (CE43) and who was 'lost' "retreating into trackless wastes" of the Essex marshes and became, Hind claims, a client king.

VIII: "a perpetuall...", Virginia Company *Records* vol. 1, 1622. [By 1685 the Powhatans of the Chesapeake tidelands were reportedly 'extinct'].

"(save upward...", William Bradford, first Governor of Plymouth, New England, 1620, *Of Plymouth Plantation*. [It is, perhaps, worth noting here: "Americans are insensible to the wonders of nature ... and may be said not to perceive the mighty forests that surround them till they fall beneath the hatchet ... their eyes are fixed on subduing nature", Alexis de Tocqueville, *Democracy in America*, 1835. Also: "America was the achievement by which Europe most truly revealed her own nature." —Fernand Braudel]

TWO

I: "Hole Haven...", inlet on the Thames estuary 'traditionally serving as a minor harbour for sea-going vessels' (Bingley). A place much visited, especially its *Lobster Smack Inn*, by the novelist Joseph Conrad's lifelong friend G.W.F. Hope, who along with Conrad lived at one time in Stanford-le-Hope, an Essex village on the banks of the Thames a couple of miles from Hole Haven. Hope, in his *Friend of Conrad* (1926), describes it: "The next day we went aboard the Nellie, taking with us a cold leg of lamb ... we got down to the Lower Hope reach. We passed several sailing ships and steamers as we made our way down to Hole Haven. When we got near the Haven I told Conrad I would take the foresail in and to keep her well down to the sea wall so as not to run any risk of touching the spit as we approached the creek. We had a fair wind in, so I lowered the main sail and took in the mizzen. We then ran up above the jetty, and let go the anchor just inside the eel schoots. We then stowed the sails and brought forth the lamb". In Hope's manuscript he identifies himself as the 'Director' in Conrad's *Heart of Darkness*, an extract from which precedes this description.

II: *Der Angriff*, newspaper published by Joseph Goebbels.

Robert Conway, main protagonist in the Frank Capra film, *Lost Horizon*, 1937.

"that nobly...", Charles White, *An Account of the Regular Graduations in Man*, 1799 [White in his account was referring to Europeans].

V: "For a...", Eric J. Dolin, *Fur, Fortune and Empire*.
"beaver fields...", *Jesuits Relations*, 1635 [from an estimated population of 60+ million beavers].
"washed up...", Roland Challis, *Shadow of a Revolution*. Quoted in John Pilger, *The New Rulers of the World*. [One million died in US/British encouraged and assisted coup in Indonesia 1965-6. "One of the worst mass murders of the 20th century" according to a CIA report. Also quoted: Richard Nixon, 1967. "With its 100 million people and its 300 mile arc of islands containing the region's richest hoard of natural resources, Indonesia is the greatest prize in South-East Asia."]
"cheap little...", John Gray, describing the faith in market economics, in a book review in *The Guardian*, 2011

VI: This entire section indebted to J.F. Hind's *A Plautius' Campaign in Britain. An Alternative Reading of the Narrative in Cassius Dio (60.19.5-21.2)*
"in avia...", retreating into trackless wastes, *op. cit.*
"REG MAG...", Great King in Britain, *op. cit.*
"reges et...", compliant, friendly kings, *op. cit.*
[It is worth noting: "Rome consistently supported the rich against the poor in all foreign communities that fell under its sway", Arnold Toynbee, *America and the World Revolution*, 1962.]

VII: "aguish miasma", William Gibbens, *The Essex Review*, 1902.

VIII: "Big swinging...", term denoting a City of London floor trader.
"A culture...", Adair Turner, Financial Services Authority, London, June 2012.
"A cesspit", Vince Cable, Business Secretary, UK government, June 2012.

IX: "cultivated...", Eduardo Galeano, *Open Veins of Latin America*. ["The powerful who legitimate their privileges by heredity cultivate nostalgia."]

"swear all...", Roland Huntford, *Shackleton*. [Referring to Robert Falcon Scott].

"Profound hypocrisy", Karl Marx, *The First Indian War of Independence 1857-9*. ["The profound hypocrisy and inherent barbarism of bourgeois civilisation ... turning from its home, where it assumes respectable forms, to the colonies,where it goes naked."]

X: "From le...", circa 1263, Randal Bingley, *op. cit.* [Hole Haven was also known as Holy Haven.]

"in very...", *National Archives*, United Kingdom. [Relating to "purged" Kenya files. Those involved in such purging were required to be "a British subject of *European descent.*"] Italics mine.

"perambulation", Randal Bingley, *op. cit.*

"by the...", an unnamed settler of the *Kenyan Police Reserve* who participated in a Special Branch interrogation: "Stayed for a few hours to help the boys out, softening him up...". Interviewed and cited by C. Elkins, *Britain's Gulag: the Brutal End of Empire in Kenya*. [cf Marx: "the universal existence of torture as a financial institution of British India" *op. cit.*]

"Bounds of...", Randal Bingley, *op. cit.* [cf Richard Drayton, *Nature's Government*: "Before territory could be consecrated as private property, or taxed, it had to be bounded, and its advantages assessed."]

"might embarrass...", Ian MacLeod, UK Secretary of State for the Colonies, 1961.

"he died...", C. Elkins, *op. cit.*

www.ingramcontent.com/pod-product-compliance
Lightning Source LLC
Chambersburg PA
CBHW021949040426
42448CB00008B/1312